ARNOLFINI

S
C
A
L
A

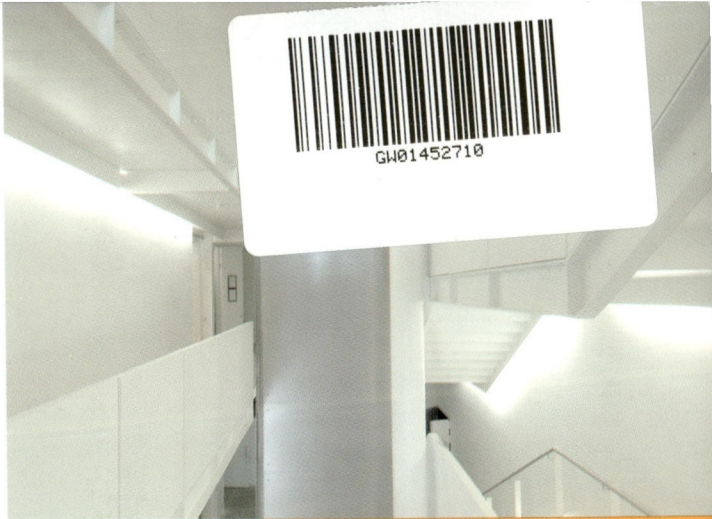

Arnolfini

Phil Johnson · ART SPACES

◀ Arnolfini entrance in 1993.

Foreword

Arnolfini was started by Jeremy Rees, Annabel Lawson and John Orsborn in 1961 and its spirit owes much to that radical decade. The organisation has adapted itself to changing circumstances and will continue to change: its purpose has remained intact. It was created for all the contemporary arts to coexist and interact in order to stimulate creativity, to provoke thought and to give pleasure to a wide range of people. Arnolfini is international in outlook, progressive in ethos and linked to the city in which it has grown.

This little book is published on the occasion of the reopening to the public of Arnolfini's building after a two-year development project. It summarises the history of Arnolfini's first 44 years, its various homes in Bristol and the refurbishments of its base since 1975.

We would like to thank the writer, journalist and music promoter Phil Johnson for his text. We acknowledge Arnolfini's debt to the research carried out by Roland Adburgham, an Arnolfini Trustee, in the preparation of his book *Under the Sky* on the history of the JT Group, whose co-founder, John Pontin, enabled Arnolfini to move to Bush House in Bristol's former docks.

We would like to thank the Design Team of the 2005 refurbishment (led by architect Robin Snell and artist Susanna Heron) and the builder, Cowlin Construction. We are grateful to the funders of the project and to Arnolfini's Trustees and staff, who have worked tirelessly to bring about the renewal of the building and its reopening in September, on the eve of its thirtieth anniversary in Bush House. Arnolfini will continue to be a public space for the imagination to take flight.

Jonathan Harvey
Chairman, Arnolfini

▶ Summer 2003, on the quayside outside Arnolfini. The animal signposts are by the artist Julian Opie, commissioned on the occasion of the opening of Baltic, Gateshead in 2002.

Down on the Docks: The History of Arnolfini's Building, Bush House

"Tunstall was excited about the event, down on the docks, a new gallery/bookshop/ coffee bar with a flash moniker, the Arnolfini…"
— Iain Sinclair, *Landor's Tower* (Granta Books, 2001)

Unlike the majority of public galleries and arts institutions throughout the world, Arnolfini in Bristol is named not after a munificent benefactor or civic worthy, but after a painting. *The Arnolfini Portrait* of 1434 by Jan van Eyck, in London's National Gallery, is one of the most famous and enigmatic images in the history of art. In 1961, the title was appropriated by Arnolfini's visionary founder Jeremy Rees to provide the memorable if obscure name for a brave new project that was to become — after a long and peripatetic journey — one of Europe's leading centres for contemporary art, visual culture and performance.

ARNOLFINI

ARNOLFINI

◀ The painting from which Arnolfini takes its name: Jan van Eyck (active 1422; died 1441), *The Arnolfini Portrait*. Oil on wood, 81.8 x 59.7 cm.

▶ Tate Modern, London.

▶ Baltic, Gateshead.

Following Arnolfini's 1975 move to its present home, Bush House, the project helped to transform Bristol itself, drawing the living centre of the city back into the harbourside, the decayed industrial buildings and redundant docks of its once grand maritime past. Like Guggenheim in Bilbao, Tate Modern in London, and Baltic in Gateshead, all of which it preceded by nearly twenty years, Arnolfini in Bristol became an agent for social and economic, as well as cultural, renewal. What began as a modest proposal to create a new, progressive venue for the arts ended up contributing to a major change in the character of the city.

The story of how Arnolfini came to be founded will be dealt with later, but the name is significant enough to provide a useful starting point. Jeremy Rees had seen *The Arnolfini Portrait* in the National Gallery on visits to London from his home in Somerset when he was a boy, and he liked it. While studying at the London College of Printing in the latter half of the 1950s, Rees published two volumes of essays, drawings and lithographs by the Polish artists Josef Herman and Marek Zulawski. For his imprint, he chose the name of Jan Arnolfini Press. When, shortly afterwards, a home was found in Bristol for the art

gallery Rees and his friends, Annabel Lawson (later Mrs Jeremy Rees) and John Orsborn, had dreamed of establishing in their home city, the problem of what to call it arose.

"Finding a suitable name for the planned new gallery proved difficult," Rees recalled in a paper written in the year 2000, three years before his tragic death, at the age of 66, in a traffic accident. "Finally, Arnolfini was chosen – as a name that people would remember, even if they mispelt it. It is fascinating to see how, and in what variety of contexts, reference is made to that van Eyck painting."

Jeremy Rees was sensitive to queries about the name, once even going so far as to add an item in an Arnolfini Newsletter disclaiming any symbolic intentions. But the name has stuck and one or two obvious associations deserve to be noted. Significantly for the context of the arts centre named after it, *The Arnolfini Portrait* is an ambiguous, reflexive work that invites a multiplicity of interpretations. It is even possible to read the physical presence of the artist within the painting itself; he may be one of two figures seen reflected in a convex mirror in the background (a Latin inscription in the wall above the mirror translates as

◀ Bristol Docks in the 1830s, as seen from Redcliffe Parade. Bush House can be made out through the masts of the tall-ships in the centre of the picture.

▶ Bush House as seen from Hannover Quay.

"Jan van Eyck has been here"). If one had to select a single image to emphasise the ludic complexity of works of art, *The Arnolfini Portrait* would suit the task perfectly. Clearly, complexity was not something the new Arnolfini would shy away from.

According to the National Gallery, the male figure in *The Arnolfini Portrait* "is probably Giovanni di Nicolao Arnolfini, a member of a wealthy Italian merchant family. He lived in Bruges in the Low Countries." Giovanni Arnolfini's status as a merchant is an important point, for Bristol is a merchant city which since medieval times has derived its money and built its monuments from the proceeds of worldwide trade, including the slave trade, the great source of mercantile wealth in the eighteenth century.

The renaissance context also finds a chance echo in the striking architectural design of Arnolfini's home from 1975 onwards, an early 19th century warehouse whose magnificently robust dimensions, and classical, plain-featured façades suggest the model of an Italian palazzo. Standing four-square on its commanding corner site overlooking the Floating Harbour – the old working-dockland setting of what

- Statue of John Cabot, who sailed from Bristol in 1497 to Newfoundland on the Canadian coast.
- Letter and invoice headers for Acramans, the original owners of the building later named Bush House.

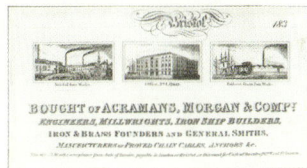

has now become Bristol's Harbourside leisure quarter – Bush House looks westward, out towards the world beyond, like the bronze civic statue of the explorer John Cabot – another Italianate Bristolian – that sits on the cobbled quay just outside Arnolfini's entrance.

Nikolaus Pevsner, in *The Buildings of England* series, describes Bush House as as "a big Bristolian warehouse in the Rundbogenstil built remarkably early. It is shown in a drawing dated 1847. Its original purpose was the storing of tea." In fact, as Andrew Foyle shows in his updated volume on Bristol for the Pevsner Architectural Guides series (Yale, 2004),

Bush House is all the more remarkable for being significantly earlier than Pevsner gave it credit for.

Designed by the architect Richard Shackleton Pope in 1830 as a warehouse and offices for Acraman's Ironworks of Narrow Quay, it turns out to be the most significant precursor of the celebrated 'Bristol Byzantine' style, epitomised by Ponton and Gough's Granary (1869) on Welsh Back – once a possible site for Arnolfini's relocation. Pope was also the architect of the Wool Hall (1828) on St Thomas Street in nearby Redcliffe, and, possibly, of Zion Congregational Chapel in Bedminster (1828–30),

◄ The Granary on Welsh Back, the epitome of the 'Bristol Byzantine' style of which Bush House was a precursor.

▶ Detail of Bush House showing the contrasting Pennant and Bath stone dressings.

both of which display similar stylistic features.

Completed by 1832, the warehouse was further extended in 1835–36 to create additional space for the storage of tea and other goods. At the time it was Bristol's largest, grandest, and most architecturally distinctive warehouse; what Foyle calls "the forefather of the Bristol Byzantine style". In 1846, ownership passed from Acraman's to George and James Bush, in whose family it remained until shortly before the Arnolfini conversion.

What is most striking about the warehouse, apart from the large, round-arched recessed windows which Pevsner related to the later German Rundboginstil, is its monumental bulk and presence. Following the 1836 extension, which added six bays to the original three of its front elevation (and created an asymmetrical appearance), the building spanned the entire corner site between Prince Street to the east and the cobbles of Narrow Quay to the west, bordering the harbour. Constructed of rough grey Pennant stone, with contrasting Bath stone dressings, its façades are much plainer than the later Byzantine warehouses that followed, where functional bulk was disguised and decorated with

◀ Narrow Quay in the 1960s, before redevelopment. Other buildings to the left of Bush House have also since been converted and now house Bristol's Architecture Centre and Youth Hostel.

fantastical, early Arts and Crafts-influenced detailing.

In 1972, the possibility arose of obtaining the warehouse for both Arnolfini and JT Building Group, a pioneering design-and-build practice set up by John Pontin, whom Jeremy Rees had met early in his career in Bristol, and who was to become Arnolfini's ally and enabler. The building, which had been threatened with partial demolition to accommodate a proposed new road, was standing empty and close to dereliction. JT Group agreed to lease the building and, together with Arnolfini, to convert it into a home for both organisations.

▶ The 1975 JT conversion of Bush House.
▶ Bush House, gutted prior to the JT conversion of 1975.

The conversion of the warehouse, with the JT Project Team led by architects Mike Duckering and Roger Mortimer, took eighteen months, at a cost of just over one million pounds. Technically, it proved an extremely challenging endeavour. As a Grade II listed building the external structure was to be retained almost intact, apart from new window frames and glazed entrances, while careful cleaning of the stone façades helped to restore the classical grandeur of the original design. Internally, the building was gutted and rebuilt entirely, the wooden floors on cast iron Doric columns replaced by reinforced-concrete floor slabs, with columns supported on a foundation of new concrete piles driven through the river silt below. An extra storey with glazed mansard sides was added to the roof, and a passenger lift fitted to the Prince Street entrance to serve the offices above Arnolfini.

When, in autumn 1975, Arnolfini opened in Bush House, it attracted national and international attention. Among the many favourable reviews William Feaver, art critic at the *Observer*, called it "the grandest arts centre in the country, and probably the best appointed." Occupying 1600 square metres on the ground and first floors Arnolfini incorporated

an exemplary range of facilities. Accommodation consisted of a large single gallery on the ground floor, smaller galleries on the first floor, and an auditorium designed for the multiple uses of cinema, music and dance which spanned both levels. There was also additional space for dressing rooms, offices, a library/bookshop and an upstairs coffee bar, while the main bar-restaurant was located downstairs, accessible through its own doorway to the quayside.

Two years after Arnolfini opened its doors at Bush House, the last working shipyard in the Floating Harbour, Albion Yard, closed down. The life of Bristol's harbourside as a place of industry rather than leisure was over.

If Arnolfini at Bush House signalled the beginning of the old docks' regeneration, other initiatives soon followed. In 1978, the last transit shed to be built in Bristol – on Princes Wharf, opposite Arnolfini's bar-restaurant entrance – was turned into the new Bristol Industrial Museum, while in 1982, following its conversion by JT Group, Watershed Media Centre opened in W-shed (a former home to Arnolfini between 1973–75) on the west

side of St. Augustine's Reach across the Floating Harbour from Narrow Quay.

This offered the prospect of a dockside cultural quarter in Bristol, with the possibility of linking Watershed and Arnolfini, and their respective quaysides, by a new bridge. Backed by JT Group and by Arnolfini, who insisted that the design of the bridge should be a collaborative project between an artist and an engineer, a competition was held and the commission won by the Irish artist, Eilis O'Connell, who worked on the design with Arup and Partners. Later named after the Bristol slave-servant of a plantation owner,

Pero's Bridge, a cantilevered design with distinctive, horn-shaped counterweights to enable the bridge to swing open to let boats past, opened in 1999.

By the turn of the millennium, Bristol's harbour-side had been transformed, with new buildings erected on the derelict Canon's Marsh site for Lloyds TSB (1990), and for the lottery-funded @Bristol project (1998–2000), together with various private housing developments. The Architecture Centre, next door to Bush House on Narrow Quay, opened in 1996, while Spike Island, a collection of artists' studios built in the disused Brooke Bond tea factory

◀ Bruce McLean, Design for
  Arnolfini café-bar, 1987.
◀ Arnolfini café-bar, 1987.
▶ The 1987 refurbishment
  design team. Left to right:
  Jeremy Fry, Arnolfini Chair
  1985–92; Barry Barker,
  Arnolfini Director 1987–90;
  David Chipperfield, architect;
  Bruce McLean, artist.

near to the Floating Harbour, opened in 1998. The waterside, once almost derelict, is now thriving, with passenger ferries connecting the city from Hotwells to Brunel's Temple Meads railway station. Other planned developments include the conversion of Bristol Industrial Museum into a new Museum of Bristol, scheduled to open in 2009.

Arnolfini had also undergone its own, minor, transformation towards the end of the 1980s, when the then Director Barry Barker commissioned architect David Chipperfield to complete a refurbishment of Arnolfini at Bush House. The most exciting and innovative aspect of a relatively modest remodelling proved to be the brilliant new interior for the bar-restaurant, designed in partnership with the artist Bruce McLean, who was invited to re-invent the bar for the 2005 refurbishment of Bush House by Snell Associates. At the time, the critic Mel Gooding described McLean's work as, "making a complex and comic statement… a set of implicit values and ideas that places art in the space of real life on the floor of the house, in the rooms where we live."

Other aspects of the 1987 Chipperfield refurbishment included the creation of a new, waterside-fronted gallery to replace the bookshop on the ground floor, and an emphatically contemporary enhancement of the reception area and staircase, using elm, Portland stone, white marble and red carpeting to redefine the interior space. "What the changes do, extremely successfully, is to transform the image of the place," the design critic Deyan Sudjic wrote in *Blueprint*: "With his by now familiar palette of materials, fresh colours, judicious slices of timber, and witty hunks of masonry, Chipperfield has created a grown-up Arnolfini, a place which has outgrown precocious adolescence." A further refurbishment by JT Group and architect Roger Mortimer took place in 1993, restoring the bookshop to its original position on the ground floor, and creating a new gallery and education space upstairs.

By the time Arnolfini closed to prepare for the Lottery-funded refurbishment of Bush House in 2003, it had become one of the most important spaces for the arts in the UK. The world outside its doors had also changed dramatically, from redundant industrial dockside to a new waterside environment for creative industries, leisure and tourism.

- Arnolfini foundation stone.
- Arnolfini entrance, prior to the 2005 redevelopment.

ARNOLFINI
WAS CREATED IN 1961
BY JEREMY & ANNABEL REES
WITH THE ENCOURAGEMENT
AND GENEROUS PATRONAGE OF
PETER & CAROLINE BARKER-MILL

ARNOLFINI'S PURPOSE IS TO PROMOTE
INTEREST IN THE CONTEMPORARY ARTS

"Enjoy yourself!": The History of Arnolfini

"I love this place. I always leave it stimulated to make some art."
– Visitor to Arnolfini, 2002 (Annual Review 2002)

The history of Arnolfini is in part the story of its co-founder and first director, Jeremy Rees, whose interests and personality helped to shape the character of the organisation as it defined itself over the twenty-five year span of his stewardship. Much of the identity of Arnolfini as a centre for the arts, and its associations with particular artists, derives from the early days of this period, when links with other West of England institutions such as Bath Academy of Art at Corsham, Dartington Hall in Devon and the artists of St Ives in Cornwall, created a focus for the new venture.

◀ Richard Long, *River Avon Mud Circle*, exhibited at Arnolfini, 1983.

◀ Arnolfini has a vibrant education programme, collaborating on projects with both artists and audiences. In 2003, art + power, a membership organisation of disabled artists, worked together with artists Aaron Williamson, Eve Dent and Elaine Kordys on *Fresh Today*, a project that culminated with a performance 'party'.

Early associations also provided continuity. Some artists, including Howard Hodgkin, Gillian Ayres and Richard Long, were to exhibit several times over the years, while other relationships were sustained across generations. Susanna Heron, who worked on the design of the most recent Arnolfini conversion with the architect Robin Snell, first exhibited at Arnolfini in 1966. Her father, the painter Patrick Heron, had an exhibition of his late work, 'Big Paintings', at Arnolfini in 1995, shortly before his death.

The breadth of Jeremy Rees's vision led Arnolfini to engage with music, performance, poetry, film and dance as well as the visual arts, and to include displays of jewellery alongside those of fine art. Such an adventurous policy was extremely rare at the time, as were Arnolfini's commitments to business sponsorship, to partnerships, and to community and education work. Even more unusually, Arnolfini acknowledged that pleasure could be an aim in itself. "When we opened Arnolfini, I wanted an inscription above the door – Enjoy yourself!" Rees said.

In March 1961 Arnolfini opened above a bookshop on Triangle West, Bristol. The first exhibition was of works on paper by Josef Herman, and paintings by

Peter Swan, a lecturer at the West of England College of Art. Inspired by the Institute of Contemporary Arts (ICA) in London, Jeremy Rees and his two artist-partners, Annabel Lawson and Peter Orsborn, each put up one hundred pounds of their own money to lease the small space, a former joinery workshop. Rees became the unpaid Director, while Lawson and Orsborn's wife, Jenny, staffed the gallery.

Monthly exhibitions reflected links with Bath Academy of Art at Corsham, where Jeremy Rees had become a lecturer in typographic design. Under the enlightened principalship of Clifford Ellis, Corsham attracted many innovative artists, including Kenneth Armitage, Howard Hodgkin, Gillian Ayres, Henry Cliffe, Michael Craig-Martin and Robyn Denny, and both lecturers and students featured in Arnolfini's exhibitions.

Although there was no money to install a telephone, new initiatives at Triangle West started almost immediately. National Open Competitions for painting were organised in 1962 and 1963, followed by a National Open Competition for jewellery in 1965. Contemporary prints and original artworks were offered for sale, a policy reflected in the 1964

exhibition 'Paintings + Sculpture for Business + Pleasure'. Collaborations with other galleries included hosting exhibitions curated by the ICA; a joint celebration of the opening of the first Severn Bridge with the West of England College of Art, and a shared exhibition of drawings by Bridget Riley with the Bear Lane Gallery in Oxford, and Midland Group Gallery, Nottingham.

Arnolfini's exhibitions travelled to Dartington Hall and other arts centres in the south west, while the 1968 show New British Sculpture involved work being sited across Bristol city centre; the subsequent Peter Stuyvesant City Sculpture Project (directed by Jeremy Rees and curated by Anthony Stokes) placed two commissions in each of eight British cities. An innovative approach to graphic design, inspired by Rees's expertise in typography and publishing, led to national design awards for the fledgling organisation's original posters and publicity. Together with visual art, live events were incorporated in the programme, including a visit by the Beat poet Allen Ginsberg. Limitations of space and problems with licensing at Triangle West meant that other venues normally had to be hired for such occasions. This,

together with Arnolfini's growing ambitions to extend
the conventional boundaries of an art gallery, under-
lined the need for larger premises.

By 1966, a tentative financial structure had been
established. A council of management was formed
with the artist-patrons Peter and Caroline Barker-Mill
as trustees; the Arts Council gave an annual revenue
grant and a guarantee against loss, Bristol City
Council added further support, while the Gulbenkian
Foundation contributed to the insulation of the gallery
roof, then a pressing concern. Jeremy Rees was able
to reduce his full-time teaching post at Bath Academy

of Art and devote more time to Arnolfini. In 1968, when the Barker-Mills created an endowment fund, Rees became Arnolfini's full-time, paid director.

Attempts to find another home started as early as 1965, with many false trails before the possibility of moving into Bush House arose. In 1969, JT Group offered Arnolfini a short-term lease on the first and ground floors of an empty warehouse at 45 Queen Square, close to Bush House. The new space – double the size of Triangle West – opened in January 1970. Arnolfini's three years on Queen Square saw the continued expansion of the exhibition programme,

together with the sale of jewellery, prints and cata-logues in a newly established bookshop. This period also marked the beginning of Arnolfini Music, launched with a fundraising concert of music by Michael Tippett at the nearby Theatre Royal. After the Arts Council's Contemporary Music Network was set up in 1971 Arnolfini became one of the main touring venues with events taking place regularly in the ground floor gallery.

Early in 1973, Arnolfini moved again, to W-Shed (later Watershed) on St Augustine's Reach. The larger scale of the new premises allowed Arnolfini to

◀ Arnolfini in W-Shed, 1973.

▼ Poster advertising the First
   Festival of British
   Independent Cinema, 1975.

effectively double in size again, and included a small arts cinema that could be combined with the main gallery for larger events. In 1975 the cinema, which received British Film Institute (BFI) funding, presented the 'First Festival of British Independent Cinema' which included work by David Hall, a founding member of the video art movement in Britain.

As visitor numbers increased, so Arnolfini's staff grew, with specialist co-ordinators for exhibitions, cinema and music, and managers for both the bookshop and the café-bar. Clive Adams, appointed as the new exhibitions co-ordinator in 1974, broadened the

policy to include more photography, including an early showing for Martin Parr. 'Beyond Painting and Sculpture', an Arts Council Touring Exhibition curated by the critic Richard Cork, and 'Artists Over Land', including both Richard Long and Hamish Fulton, were particularly important shows of this period.

By the time Arnolfini moved into Bush House in the autumn of 1975, its opening season was able to offer a more ambitious mix than perhaps any arts organisation in the country, with *New Paintings* by Howard Hodgkin shown alongside hybrid works by Keith Milow and photographs by Stephen Guion Williams. Elgar Howarth conducted the Grimethorpe Brass Band at the Victoria Rooms in Clifton, while the Philip Glass Ensemble performed *Music In Twelve Parts* in Arnolfini's auditorium. There were also programmes of dance, cinema and jewellery.

By the beginning of the 1980s, Arnolfini had become an essential part of the cultural landscape, with over 150,000 visitors annually. Financial stability also appeared to improve when JT Group acquired the freehold of Bush House in 1979 and Peter Barker-Mill established the Ashley Clinton Endowment Fund. A growing trend for more theoretically informed shows

was reflected in exhibitions such as *Narrative Paintings*, *Women's Images of Men*, *Objects and Sculpture* (a two-part exhibition in partnership with the ICA), *Homework* (curated by Maureen Paley) and a solo show of Susan Hiller's work.

Commitments to music and dance were strengthened, and the growing programme of educational and community activities extended to include workshops with schools and local artists' groups, as well as regular Saturday workshops for children. Collaborations with the newly opened Watershed included co-hosting *Navigations*, the Fourth National

Photography Conference, with Martha Rosler as keynote speaker, and running themed film seasons across both venues.

In July of 1985, Arnolfini presented one of its most popular shows, *Graffiti Art*, which also secured it a place in the history of what was to become known as 'the Bristol Sound'. A group of graffiti artists, including 3D (Robert Del Naja, later of Massive Attack), were commissioned to spray work directly onto the gallery walls, and for a linked event Arnolfini asked The Wild Bunch, the Bristol sound system out of which Massive Attack and the record

▶ Magdalena Jetelovà, *Place*, one of the works on the Forest of Dean Sculpture Trail.

producer Nellee Hooper emerged, to perform in the downstairs gallery. A video document of the event records the presence of many of the Bristol musicians who would later go on to worldwide fame.

In 1986, Jeremy Rees and exhibitions co-ordinator Rupert Martin, in conjunction with Martin Orrom of the Forestry Commission, established the Forest of Dean Sculpture Trail in Gloucestershire. Over 20 works, both permanent and temporary, by sculptors including Cornelia Parker, Peter Randall-Page, David Nash and Ian Hamilton-Finlay, were sited on a three and a half mile trail through the ancient forest. Like the transformation of Bristol's harbourside, begun by the conversion of Bush House, the Forest of Dean Sculpture Trail became a landmark development in the planning of new environmental initiatives for arts and leisure tourism. It remains a permanent, and beautiful achievement.

It was at this point in the mid-1980s, however, that Arnolfini – in common with many arts organisations in the Thatcher years – experienced serious problems with funding. Grants from the Arts Council and South West Arts suffered slight cuts in an era of rising inflation, and when the BFI cut its grant by half,

a crisis developed. The organisation that Jeremy Rees had created, a space where a range of contemporary art forms could be presented, became, in effect, a victim of its ambition. Arnolfini was forced to retrench, the commitment to jewellery ended, the innovative Video Library closed and the role of music was reduced in order that the organisation could go forward. In 1985, Peter Barker-Mill, then aged 70, stood down as chair of the trustees, to be replaced in 1986 by Jeremy Fry. In the autumn of 1986, Jeremy Rees resigned. "In all my time here, my one and only regret has been that the city and county have failed to make a realistic contribution to what has, in effect, been a public service," he told *Venue*, the local listings magazine.

Barry Barker, appointed Director in 1987, commissioned the refurbishment by architect David Chipperfield. His previous experience as Director of Exhibitions at ICA and Director of the John Hansard Gallery in Southampton informed a series of shows that marked a high point in terms of exhibitions, including work by artists such as Joseph Beuys, Juan Muñoz, Alastair MacLennan, Gillian Ayres and Guiseppe Penone.

He left Arnolfini in 1990 to take charge of the National Touring Exhibitions programme at the South Bank Centre and was succeeded by Tessa Jackson in 1991. During her eight-year tenure she, together with Jonathan Harvey as Chairman of the Board, successfully re-established financial stability and restored balance to the programme, before leaving to become Director of the Scottish Arts Council.

Reflecting changes in art practice as a whole, Arnolfini devoted more attention to video art (first shown in 1981's *Expanded Video Show*), performance and installation. A Live Art department was established whose commitments to experimental dance and theatre continued in the founding spirit of Arnolfini. Working in partnership with the University of Bristol and the Chicago-based performance collective Goat Island, Arnolfini Live hosted a series of summer schools and symposia. This, together with commissioning initiatives such as *Breathing Space* and *Method Lab* and the biennial festival *Inbetween Time*, initiated in 2001, reflect their success.

As Caroline Collier replaced Tessa Jackson in 1999, a new phase was initiated. An ambitious programme of exhibitions, linked conferences and

◄ Part of the exhibition
*renovation filter: recent
past and near future*
by Liam Gillick, 2000.

► Victor Burgin, *Listen to
Britain*, 2002 (video still),
exhibited at Arnolfini in the
same year.

events placed increasing emphasis on cross-disciplinary approaches, and on artistic practice with a marked intellectual or philosophical dimension, evident in important exhibitions devoted to Vito Acconci, Eleanor Antin, Michael Snow, Victor Burgin and Gina Pane.

Arnolfini continued to showcase new and emerging artists, including David Musgrave and Janice Kerbel, to put on exhibitions of influential artists such as Liam Gillick, and to collaborate with guest curators and other local and national partner-institutions, as in the shared initiative with Spike Island in 2001, *The Silk Purse Procedure*. The touring and publication programmes continued to develop, and the bookshop – an important part of the life of the organisation since the Queen Square period – initiated a successful programme of readings and events. Ed Lewis programmed Arnolfini's cinema between 1991 and his untimely death in 2003. He continued a long tradition of showing quality art house film punctuated with the often quirky and perennially popular 'double bills' he had pioneered at London's Riverside Studios. Where else could you enjoy the unlikely pairing of *Breakdance* and *Fame*

◀ *Raptor*, Dalziel & Scullion, *Flock on Film*, part of the *Commotion* artists' film programme shown at Arnolfini in 2003.
▶ Arnolfini, Narrow Quay.

within an experimental dance season? During this period a new programme of artists' films, *Commotion*, was initiated with the Bristol-based organisation Picture This, whose Director, Josephine Lanyon, had worked at Arnolfini as Exhibitions Officer between 1994 and 1998.

However, the growing limitations of the physical environment at Bush House – inaccessibility, poor lighting, low ceilings, insufficient technical space, inadequate atmospheric controls and circulation between spaces – had led the trustees and Director Tessa Jackson, as early as 1997, to begin to plan a major capital development project to be funded by the National Lottery, a process that would take several years. Its eventual success helped Arnolfini to buy the freehold of Bush House and to plan a new phase of development that would allow Jeremy Rees's founding vision of an organisation for all the arts, and for everyone, to be renewed.

◀ Outline floor plans for
Arnolfini's 2003–05
redevelopment project.
▶ A cross section illustrating
the layout of the new design.

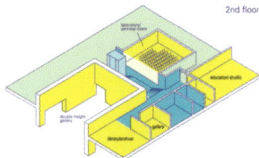

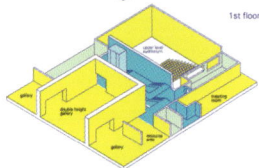

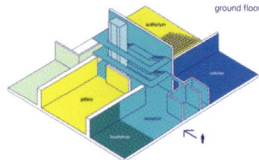

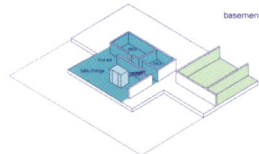

Arnolfini's Development: A Renewal of Spaces

"With its mix of visual and performing arts and its focus on experimentation and education, Arnolfini is already unique in the English regions. The new designs will enable the organisation to take its place as one of a handful of the most significant contemporary cultural centres in Europe."
– Nicholas Serota, Director, Tate

In July 1999, as part of an exhibition entitled Quay Designs, Arnolfini presented its initial plans for the remodelling of Bush House. Architect Robin Snell of Snell Associates and artist Susanna Heron had been working on the development with project manager John Monahan since 1998. The exhibition set Arnolfini within its waterfront context and featured the parallel developments of Explore (Chris Wilkinson Architects) and Wildscreen (Michael Hopkins and Partners), part of the @Bristol complex on the Canon's Marsh site across the Floating Harbour from Bush House. These projects continued the

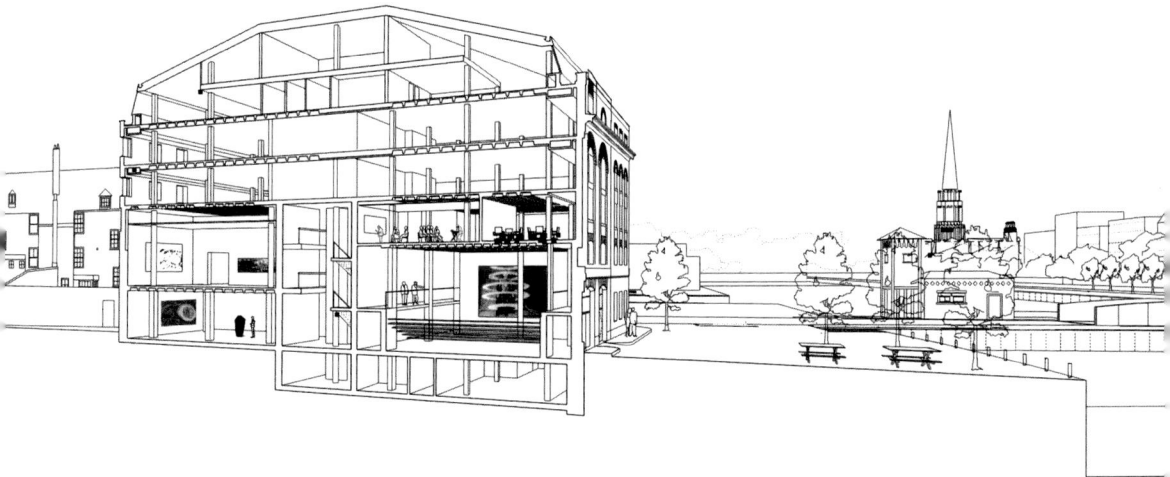

▶ Work begins on refurbishing Arnolfini, September 2003.

process of redefining the environment of Bristol's harbourside and the once derelict docks, begun by the original Arnolfini conversion of Bush House in 1975. As one of six British cities shortlisted for the title of 2008 European City of Culture (awarded to Liverpool in 2003), Bristol's bid placed great emphasis on this waterside complex of arts and leisure facilities, which represented a new cultural centre at the heart of the city.

In autumn 2001 Arnolfini was successful in its bid for capital funding from the Arts Council of England through the National Lottery. Following

the purchase of the freehold to Bush House the planned redevelopment was able to proceed with additional support from Bristol City Council, South West Regional Development Agency and a number of charitable trusts, foundations and individuals.

As work began on the refurbishment of Bush House at the end of September 2003, Arnolfini established *Interlude*, a programme of off-site events planned to run throughout the closure of the building. The bookshop – which was to be kept open throughout the development – was also moved to

◀ Susanna Heron,
The Sunken Courtyard,
Hackney Community College,
London, 1995–97.
▶ Arnolfini's auditorium.

a temporary building on Narrow Quay to act as an information point and box office for patrons during the construction period.

Architect Robin Snell's other projects included Fulham Football Club's new stadium in London, the Northern Architecture Centre in Newcastle and a new art gallery for the Surrey Institute of Art and Design, while Susanna Heron had worked on several notable public art projects, including *The Sunken Courtyard* for the Shoreditch campus of Hackney Community College, *Island* for the entrance to the British Embassy in Dublin, and *Slate Frieze* for the Council of the European Union in Brussels. Cowlin Construction, a Bristol firm first established in 1834 – when the original Acramans building was still being completed – became the main building contractor.

As with the original conversion in 1975, substantial engineering work was required to create the essential feature of the plan: a central open space (with a new staircase and lift), leading to the auditorium and other project spaces. A new basement level was excavated to house essential services. The new building would be fully accessible and provide what the project brief described as "exemplary spaces for

◀ Having engineered new
structural supports into
position, parts of the second
floor and existing supporting
pillars were removed in
order to create a new,
uninterrupted, double-height
gallery space.

▶ An early ground-plan sketch
by the architect Robin Snell,
illustrating the palazzo-style
design.

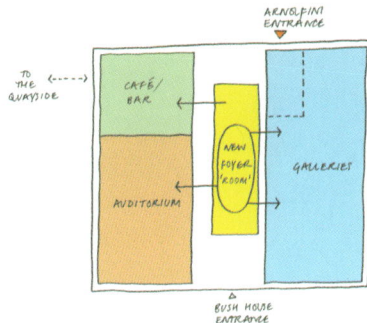

the contemporary arts – flexible white cube galleries, black box auditorium, light and dark studios, library, archive, meeting room, stimulating public space, bookshop, and café-bar."

As Arnolfini would gain an extra floor (two floors, including the basement), existing facilities could be expanded and enhanced, as with the new double-height first floor gallery. Here, the obstructions of the existing galleries' supporting pillars were removed while atmospheric controls allowed increased comfort for visitors and enabled Arnolfini to meet conditions for borrowing and displaying sensitive works of art. For the first time visitors would also be able to see the true depth of the building, with the removal of previous office accommodation allowing the public spaces and galleries to occupy the whole span of the large corner site, from Prince Street to Narrow Quay. A sense of intimacy – and a corrective to the growing trend for 'blockbuster' values within the arts generally – would be preserved by the layout's variations in scale, and by the creation of a small upstairs gallery intended for the presentation of single works of art and small-scale performance.

◄ The new multi-purpose dark studio on the second floor has been designed to accommodate sound and video work, as well as to provide rehearsal space for live art and dance artists.

► In keeping with the architect's aim to 'rediscover the quayside warehouse spirit of the building', a decision was made to retain the moulded concrete 'waffles' that were a feature of the 1975 JT redevelopment.

▶ The new central circulation space.

"The important architectural decision is to punch a hole through the centre of the plan to enable new patterns of movement through the building, or 'cross-over' between spaces allowing a new reading of the interiors and Arnolfini's activities," Robin Snell said as construction got underway. "This device also responds to the Italian palazzo-style design of the existing listed warehouse. The traditional palazzo, or urban villa, often has an internal courtyard at its heart to provide open spaces, light, ventilation and a means of ordering the rooms around the centre. The new central space at Arnolfini contains the circulation stairs, bridges and a lift which will become the key reference point within the building."

The functional character of the original Bush House would also be reflected in the interior surfaces of the new conversion. "The materials and finishes used in the redevelopment aim to rediscover the quayside warehouse spirit of the building", said Snell. "Interiors will be neutral and have an industrial quality, with exposed concrete floors running through the building, and painted concrete ceilings. The existing building has

undergone a series of refurbishments and changes over its life and the project can be seen as one of architectural renewal, a continuation of this tradition."

Susanna Heron's role in the design process reflected her working practice as an artist. "I look very hard at the nature of a place, about what it is and what it should be," she said. "It is a process of uncovering, making visible, making active that which is inherent. During the time I have worked with Arnolfini as Design Team Artist I have examined the perceptual 'bones' of the building, its physical presence, its complex function and situation." This process led to the identification of a number of specific practical areas to be addressed, including how to improve the entrance and foyer spaces in order to provide "a sense of arrival"; how to bring light, air and space into the building; and how to ensure the maximum adaptability of gallery and project spaces.

The creation of spaces suitable for the presentation and the production of art also included an artist's commission – a new café-bar by Bruce McLean and Robin Snell. The original bar, part of the 1987 refurbishment, was a collaboration between McLean and

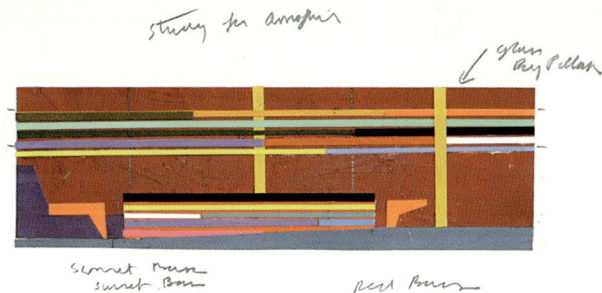

study for arnolfini

glass bay pillar

summer music
sunset Bar

Real Bar

the architect David Chipperfield. One of the earliest such collaborations, the café-bar was conceived as a work within a white cube gallery space. A similar approach has been taken in the reinvention of the café bar for the new building.

The aim of ensuring that all spaces were fully accessible was key to the whole redevelopment. Previously, without the benefit of a lift, Arnolfini remained a difficult and restrictive environment for many users. "Unless you could climb the stairs only half the building – half of an exhibition – was open to you," said Caroline Collier. "What we needed to do

was link different aspects of the programme and the spaces of the building, so that you immediately get a feel of where you are and are able to find your way around the building, hence the central circulation area and all the rooms going off that space. That's the principle, to have a layered programme which allows you either to use all the spaces for one project, or as with John Cage's idea for his music circus, to allow for simultaneous but independent activity."

The reference to John Cage is a meaningful one. The huge span of Cage's interests, from music, dance and the visual arts to philosophy and fungi, together

◀ ▶ The new staircase.

with the humanistic concerns that connected all the disparate parts into a simultaneous whole, make him a kind of secular patron saint for Arnolfini and for the development of its founding vision. His complex layering of references also provides a fitting contemporary complement to the enigmatic language of van Eyck's *The Arnolfini Portrait*. It reminds us that, in art, meaning is never as simple as it seems.

This edition © Scala Publishers Ltd, 2005
Text © Phil Johnson, 2005

First published in 2005 by
Scala Publishers Ltd
Northburgh House
10 Northburgh Street
London EC1V 0AT

ISBN 1 85759 401 0

Designed by Andrew Shoolbred and Greg Taylor
Edited by Oliver Craske
Printed in Spain
10 9 8 7 6 5 4 3 2 1

Supported by

South West *of* England
Regional Development Agency

◄◄ Front and back cover: Daytime and nighttime exterior views
of Arnolfini.

◄ Page 1: The new central circulation space at the heart of
the redeveloped Bush House.

Picture Credits

Woodley & Quick Photography: front and back cover, 2, 5, 9, 22 (right),
23, 25, 26, 27, 44, 47, 53.
Jamie Woodley: 1, 51, 54, 56, 57, 59–63.
© The National Gallery, London: 6
© Tate Photography/Andrew Dunkley: 7 (upper)
BALTIC, Don Barker, 2003: 7 (lower)
Arnolfini archive: 10, 13, 14–15, 16, 17, 18, 28, 34, 36, 37, 38
Bristol Records Office: 11
Destination Bristol: 12
Watershed: 19
www.bristol-city.gov.uk: 20–21
Piers Rawson: 29
Reproduced with kind permission of Jenny Orsborn: 30, 32
Derek Balmer: 31
British Artists' Film and Video Collection: 35
Forest of Dean Sculpture Trust: 41
Dragan Dragin: 42
Tara Molloy: 43
Courtesy of the artists/Houldsworth, London: 46
Thirteen: 48
Snell Associates: 49, 55
www.susannaheron.com: 52

Every effort has been made to acknowledge copyright of images
where applicable. Any errors or omissions are unintentional and
should be brought to the attention of the Publisher.

The publishers would like to thank Caroline Collier, Peter Begen, Helen
Pearson, Sharon Tuttle and Julian Warren for their kind assistance.